Bilingual Kids™

ENGLISH SPANISH

Lessons & Activities for Bilingual Learners
Lecciones y actividades para aprendices bilingües

By / Por
Diana Isaza
and / y
Patricia Gómez

ISBN: 1-553860-025-X

Acknowledgements / Reconocimientos

Authors / *Autoras*	Diana Isaza and / y Patricia Gómez
Illustrators / *Ilustradores*	Various contributors / Varios colaboradores
Cover Design / *Portada*	Campbell Creative Services
Editor / *Editor*	Robert Gaiero
Layout / *Diseño interior*	Patricia Gómez and / y Darryl Taylor

We suggest the purchase of our companion CD/book kit, *Bilingual Songs: English-Spanish, vol. 2*, which uses music to teach the material presented in this book.

Recomendamos la compra de nuestro CD/Book Kit, *Bilingual Songs: English-Spanish, vo2.* el cual contiene canciones que complementan y refuerzan el material presentado en cada una de estas lecciones.

For further information contact:
Para obtener mayor información:

Jordan Music Productions Inc.
M.P.O. Box 490
Niagara Falls, NY
U.S.A. 14302-0490

Jordan Music Productions Inc.
Station M, Box 160
Toronto, Ontario
Canada, M6S 4T3

Telephone: 1-800-567-7733
Website: www.sara-jordan.com
E-mail: sjordan@sara-jordan.com

Agradecemos el apoyo financiero del Gobierno de Canadá, otorgado por nuestra actividad editorial a través del programa para el desarrollo de la industria del libro (BPIDP).

We acknoledge the financial support of the Government of Canada through the Book Publishing Industry Development Program (BPIDP) for our publishing activities.

List of Skills Covered in this Book
Lista de habilidades aplicadas en este libro

Oral Communication / *Funciones comunicativas*

- the ability to follow Spanish/English instructions and suggestions
- visual and verbal skills using repetition
- the promotion of cultural exchange with native Spanish/English speakers
- the development of critical thinking skills through:

> * animated characters, making learning a real life experience

Writing / *Escritura*

- the ability to follow articulated sequences of instruction where each topic builds upon those of preceding levels
- written exercises helping students to gain an appreciation of Spanish/English cultures

Reading / *Lectura*

- reading simple material
- reading and responding to comprehension activities
- engaging in written material providing a complete learning experience:

> * answering short questions
>
> * word boxes
>
> * filling in missing words
>
> * finding secret messages
>
> * coloring activities
>
> * matching columns
>
> * drawing pictures
>
> * charts
>
> * signs
>
> * song lyrics (if used with the the corresponding
> *Bilingual Songs: English / Spanish Vol. 2* CD/Book kit)

Grammar / *Gramática*

- interrogative, affirmative and negative constructions
- nouns and pronouns
- gender of nouns in Spanish
- agreement of adjectives
- abbreviations
- prepositions
- definite article *the* in English and *el, la, los, las in Spanish*
- present tense of the verbs *to be* and *to know / ser/estar* and *conocer/saber*

Vocabulary Building / *Construcción de vocabulario*

- integrating immediate translation of new words
- using basic vocabulary such as: colors, numbers, things in the home, time expressions, calendar, family, sports, professions, etc.
- vocabulary building exercises including:
  * word scrambles
  * crosswords
  * letter soups

Spelling Words / Strategies / *Deletrear / Estrategias*

- alphabetization
- capitalization (days, months, proper names)
- punctuation (Spanish upside-down exclamation and question marks)

Standards of Foreign Language Learning*
Estándares para el aprendizaje de idiomas extranjeros

The concepts taught in this book comply with the five major organizing principles
of the "Standards of Foreign Language Learning" in the following ways:

Communication in Spanish

a) conversing providing and obtaining information; expressing feelings and emotions, and exchanging opinions
b) understanding and interpreting spoken and written Spanish
c) presenting information, concepts, and ideas in Spanish

Cultures of the World

a) understanding Hispanic cultural behaviors: gestures, oral expressions for greetings, cultural activities such as games, holidays, etc.
b) developing an awareness of products from Hispanic cultures: artesanías, papeletas, títeres, contemporary dress, children's songs, literature, and stories

Connections to Other Disciplines

a) demonstrating, in Spanish, an understanding of other subject areas such as community, professions, mathematics, and geography
b) applying knowledge of the metric system to everyday life situations
c) reading, listening to, and talking about folk tales, short stories, poems and songs in Spanish

Comparisons and Insights into the Nature of Language and Culture

a) understanding similarities and differences between English and Spanish
b) being aware of idiomatic expressions, formal and informal forms of language

Communities at Home and Abroad

a) conveying messages to Spanish speakers in person, email, letters, etc.
b) being aware of professions that benefit from knowing Spanish
c) performing skits and songs in Spanish for school and community celebrations like Cinco de Mayo
d) becoming life-long learners by using Spanish for enrichment and enjoyment: cuentos infantiles, children's web pages, children's programs, latin music, games like Dominó and La Gallina Ciega.
e) establishing friendships within the local Spanish-speaking community.

*Adapted from the National Standards in Foreign Language Education, a collaborative project of ACTFL, AATF & AATSP.

Table of Contents
Tabla de contenido

Themes / Temas

Tips for Teachers and Parents
Sugerencias para profesores y padres de familia

1. Begin by teaching students to recognize that Spanish nouns are either feminine and masculine. Students should also recognize the corresponding articles and their forms. Example: *el, la, los, las, uno, una*
2. Introduce the new characters Juan and Joe to your students. They will help them to learn Spanish and English.
3. Repeat the sentences several times so that students can learn correct pronunciation.
4. Icons, like the ones shown below, will differentiate between lesson and activity pages.

1. *Empiece por enseñar a los estudiantes a reconocer las dos formas de las palabras en español: femeninas y masculinas. Además los estudiantes deberán reconocer el artículo correspondiente a estas dos formas.*
2. *Presente a los estudiantes los nuevos personajes Juan y Joe. Ellos les ayudarán a aprender español e inglés*
3. *Repita las oraciones varias veces para que los estudiantes aprendan la pronunciación.*
4. *Las siguientes señales le indicarán si el tema es una lección o una actividad.*

Lesson
Lección

Activity
Actividad

¡Hola! Soy Juan.

Hello! I'm Joe.

This book has been designed for teaching both English and Spanish. Instructions are given in both languages. However, receiving instructions in one's native language can be advantageous when completing exercises written in the language that is being learned. For even better results, we recommend the use of the companion resource *Bilingual Songs: English-Spanish, vol. 2* which complements and reinforces the lessons learned here.

1. Gender / *El género*

In Spanish, all nouns (person, place, thing or idea) are either masculine or feminine.

1. Nouns that end in <u>o</u> are usually masculine.
   Most nouns that end in <u>a</u> are feminine.

2. *El* and *la* both mean **the**. Use the article *el* with masculine nouns and *la* with feminine nouns.

*En inglés, los sustantivos no tienen género. Se usa **the** en todos los casos.*

Masculine / *Masculino*   Feminine / *Femenino*

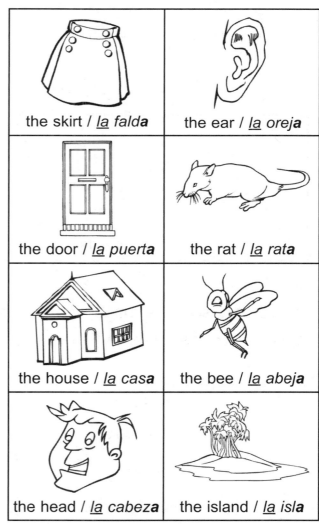

the shoe / <u>el</u> zapat**o**   the duck / <u>el</u> pat**o**

the hat / <u>el</u> sombrer**o**   the car / <u>el</u> aut**o**

the arm / <u>el</u> braz**o**   the pig / <u>el</u> cerd**o**

the finger / <u>el</u> ded**o**   the echo / <u>el</u> ec**o**

the skirt / <u>la</u> fald**a**   the ear / <u>la</u> orej**a**

the door / <u>la</u> puert**a**   the rat / <u>la</u> rat**a**

the house / <u>la</u> cas**a**   the bee / <u>la</u> abej**a**

the head / <u>la</u> cabez**a**   the island / <u>la</u> isl**a**

3. In Spanish, the gender of people or animals depends upon their sex.
   En español, el género en humanos y animales depende del sexo.

Masculine / *Masculino*

the boy/ *el niño* | the uncle / *el tío* | the bear/ *el oso* | the cat / *el gato*

Feminine / *Femenino*

the girl / *la niña* | the aunt / *la tía* | the bear / *la osa* | the cat / *la gata*

4. In other cases, the masculine and feminine forms are different words.
   En otros casos, el femenino y el masculino son palabras diferentes.

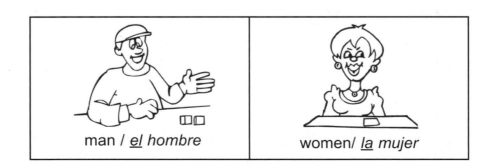

man / *el hombre* | women/ *la mujer*

Bilingual Kids: English-Spanish, Vol. 2   © 2005 Sara Jordan Publishing

5. Some nouns have the same form for both genders. In this case, the gender is indicated by the article: <u>el</u> or <u>la</u>, <u>un</u> or <u>una</u>.

   Algunos nombres utilizan la misma forma para ambos géneros.
   En este caso el género lo indica el artículo : <u>el</u> o <u>la</u>, <u>un</u> o <u>una</u>.

| student / <u>el</u> estudiante | student / l<u>a</u> estudiante |

6. The letters of the alphabet are feminine.
   Las letras del alfabeto son del género femenino.

   <u>la</u> a   <u>la</u> m   <u>la</u> z

7. Days of the week, colors, and numbers are masculine.
   Los días de la semana, los colores y los números son masculinos.

Monday / <u>el</u> lunes	green / <u>el</u> verde	nine / <u>el</u> nueve
Tuesday / <u>el</u> martes	blue / <u>el</u> azul	five / <u>el</u> cinco
Wednesday / <u>el</u> miércoles	red / <u>el</u> rojo	thirteen / <u>el</u> trece

Name / Nombre

Activity 1 / *Actividad 1*

a. Write the article that corresponds to each word.

   Escribe el artículo que corresponde a cada palabra.

__ __ eme

__ __ ocho

__ __ *rojo*
__ __ *amarillo*
__ __ *verde*

__ __ *mujer*

__ __ sombrero

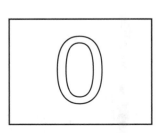

__ __ cero

__ __ luna

__ __ eñe

__ __ lunes

Bilingual Kids: English-Spanish, Vol. 2   © 2005 Sara Jordan Publishing

Activity 2 / *Actividad 2*

a. Fill in the puzzle squares with the Spanish word for each picture.

   Llena los espacios con la palabra en español.

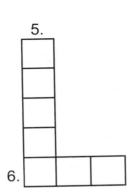

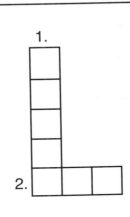

b. Fill in the blanks with the appropriate vowel or article.

   Completa con la letra final o el artículo.

la   arañ___   el   zapat__

____   mesa   __ __   auto

Choo! Choo! Count!

¡Chu! ¡Chu! ¡Cuenta!

1 one *uno*	**2** two *dos*	**3** three *tres*	**4** four *cuatro*	**5** five *cinco*
6 six *seis*	**7** seven *siete*	**8** eight *ocho*	**9** nine *nueve*	**10** ten *diez*
11 eleven *once*	**12** twelve *doce*	**13** thirteen *trece*	**14** fourteen *catorce*	**15** fifteen *quince*

Bilingual Kids: English-Spanish, Vol. 2 © 2005 Sara Jordan Publishing

2. Counting to 30 / *Contando hasta 30*

16 sixteen *dieciséis*	**17** seventeen *diecisiete*	**18** eighteen *dieciocho*	**19** nineteen *diecinueve*	**20** twenty *veinte*
21 twenty-one *veintiuno*	**22** twenty-two *veintidós*	**23** twenty-three *veintitrés*	**24** twenty-four *veinticuatro*	**25** twenty-five *veinticinco*
26 twenty-six *veintiséis*	**27** twenty-seven *veintisiete*	**28** twenty-eight *veintiocho*	**29** twenty-nine *veintinueve*	**30** thirty *treinta*

Name / Nombre

Activity 1 / *Actividad 1*

a. *Organiza los números en inglés*

wto

_____

oruf

_____

tetywn-noe

_____

yirhtt

_____

b. Unscramble the Spanish numbers.

eteis

_____

eveuntivein

_____

ceinqu

_____

inattre

_____

Bilingual Kids: English-Spanish, Vol. 2   © 2005 Sara Jordan Publishing

2. Counting to 30 / *Contando hasta 30*

Activity 2 / *Actividad 2*

Complete the addition exercises and illustrate them.
Write the numbers in Spanish.

Dibuja y suma los elementos en cada conjunto.
Escribe el número en inglés

strawberries / *fresas*

ocho / eight 8 + *seis* / six 6

= *catorce* / fourteen 14

spoons / *cucharas*

_____ 3 + _____ 9

= _____ ☐

bees / *abejas*

_____ 13 + _____ 7

= _____ ☐

books / *libros*

_____ 5 + _____ 8

= _____ ☐

Olympic Counting by Tens

Let's go to the Olympics and learn to count by tens from 10 to 100.

Suggestion: photocopy pages 18 and 19 for the class. Have them cut out the "Olympic" cards. Mix them up and then sort them in order.

ten
diez

twenty
veinte

thirty
treinta

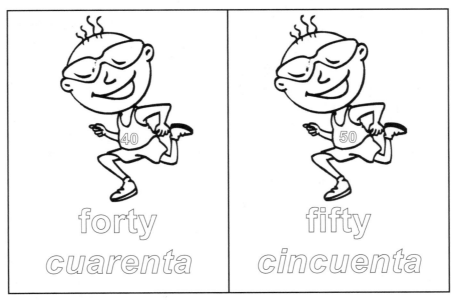

forty
cuarenta

fifty
cincuenta

Bilingual Kids: English-Spanish, Vol. 2 © 2005 Sara Jordan Publishing

3. Counting by Tens / *Contando por decenas*

Contando por decenas en los Juegos Olímpicos

Vamos a los Juegos Olímpicos y aprendamos a contar por decenas desde el 10 hasta el 100.

Sugerencia: fotocopie las páginas 18 y 19. Haga que los alumnos corten las tarjetas de los Juegos Olímpicos. Mezclenlas para luego ubicarlas en orden.

Name / Nombre

Activity 1 / *Actividad 1*

Find the multiples of ten in Spanish and in English.

Encuentra los múltiplos de diez en español y en inglés.

T	E	N	S	E	T	E	N	T	A	X	O	O
T	R	E	I	N	T	A	Z	N	E	I	C	N
S	E	V	E	N	T	Y	B	W	C	F	H	E
C	I	N	C	U	E	N	T	A	A	T	E	H
Q	G	D	Y	V	T	H	I	R	T	Y	N	U
M	H	K	L	N	W	R	L	P	N	N	T	N
S	T	N	I	N	E	T	Y	B	E	O	A	D
X	Y	H	R	F	N	G	Q	P	R	V	Y	R
S	E	S	E	N	T	A	S	D	A	E	T	E
Z	F	O	R	T	Y	X	W	R	U	N	F	D
S	E	T	N	I	E	V	I	F	C	T	I	W
D	I	E	Z	S	Y	T	X	I	S	A	F	G

3. Counting by Tens / *Contando por decenas*

Name / Nombre

Activity 2 / *Actividad 2*

Look at the pictures and write the corresponding numbers in English and Spanish.

Observa las imágenes y escribe el número correspondiente en inglés y en español.

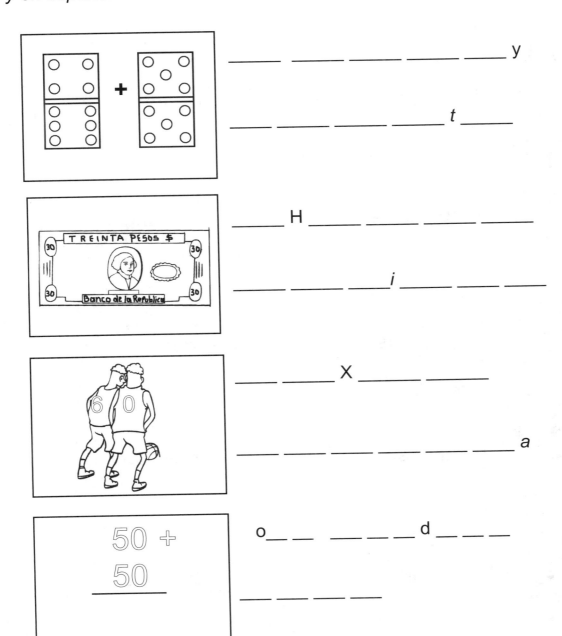

_____ _____ _____ _____ y

_____ _____ _____ _____ *t* _____

_____ H _____ _____ _____ _____

_____ _____ *i* _____ _____ _____

_____ _____ X _____ _____ _____

_____ _____ _____ _____ _____ *a*

o_____ _____ _____ *d* _____ _____

_____ _____ _____ _____

Did you know that traffic signs are used around the world to guide, inform and warn us? Let's learn their shapes.

¿Sabías que las señales de tráfico son usadas en todo el mundo para guiarnos, informarnos y prevenirnos? Aprendamos sus formas.

	circle	*el círculo*
	rectangle	*el rectángulo*
	rhombus	*el rombo*
	square	*el cuadrado*
	triangle	*el triángulo*

Bilingual Kids: English-Spanish, Vol. 2   © 2005 Sara Jordan Publishing

5. Emotions / *Las emociones*

Activity 1 / *Actividad 1*

How are they feeling? Choose the correct words from word box and write the entire sentences in English and Spanish.

¿Cómo están ellos? Escoje las palabras correctas de la parte inferior de la página y escribe las oraciones completas en inglés y en español

_____

_____

_____

_____

_____

_____

_____

_____

a. You / happy	a. *Tú / feliz*
b. He / angry	b. *Él / enojado*
c. We / bored	c. *Nosotros / aburridos*
d. They / surprised	d. *Ellos / sorprendidos*

Name / Nombre

Activity 2 / *Actividad 2*

Complete each sentence with an emotion and draw illustrations
in the boxes provided.

Completa cada oración con la emoción correspondiente.
Dibuja cada expresión.

a. At home I am _____.

a. *En mi casa estoy _____.*

b. At school we are _____.

b. *En la escuela estamos _____.*

c. My teacher is _____.

c. *Mi maestro(a) está _____.*

d. At the circus the clowns are _____.

d. *En el circo los payasos están _____.*

Bilingual Kids: English-Spanish, Vol. 2 © 2005 Sara Jordan Publishing

Color the farm / *Colorea la granja*

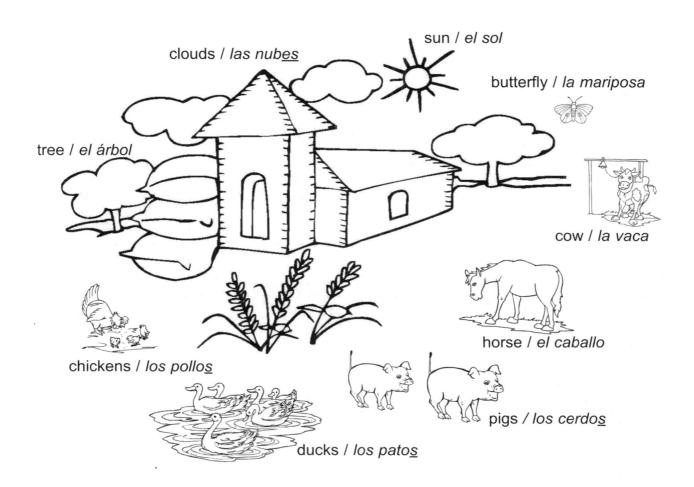

Spanish singular nouns are made plural by adding **s** to words ending in a vowel and **es** to words ending in a consonant. Don't forget to change **el** to **los** for masculine plural and **la** to **las** for feminine plural.

El plural de la mayoría de las palabras en inglés se forma agregando **s** *al final. Palabras comunes terminadas en ch, sh, s, ss, x, z o zz forman el plural agregando* **es**. *Otras palabras cambian al formar el plural como:* foot - feet, man - men, mouse - mice, woman - women, tooth - teeth.

Name / Nombre

Activity 1 / *Actividad 1*

Let's practice! Make the following words plural in Spanish.

¡Practiquemos! Escribe el plural de las siguientes palabras en español.

pig / el *cerdo*

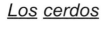
Los cerdos

horse / el *caballo*

_____

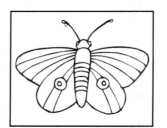

butterfly / la *mariposa*

_____

sun / *el sol*

_____

cow / la *vaca*

_____

tree / el *árbol*

_____

flower / la *flor*

_____

hen / la *gallina*

_____

duck / el *pato*

_____

Bilingual Kids: English-Spanish, Vol. 2   © 2005 Sara Jordan Publishing

6. The Countryside / *El campo*

Name / Nombre

Activity 2 / *Actividad 2*

In each group, color the animal which produces any kind of food and lives in the countryside.

En cada grupo, colorea el animal que vive en el campo y nos proporciona algún alimento.

a.

b.

c.

Many adults in our community work to make our lives better.
What would you like to do when you grow up?

Muchos adultos en nuestra comunidad trabajan para hacer más agradable y segura nuestra vida.
¿Qué te gustaría ser cuando grande?

doctor

el doctor
la doctora

driver

el conductor
la conductora

librarian

el bibliotecario
la bibliotecaria

journalist

el / la periodista

baker

el panadero
la panadera

shopkeeper

el tendero
la tendera

policeman
policewoman

el / la policía

gardener

el jardinero
la jardinera

Bilingual Kids: English-Spanish, Vol. 2   © 2005 Sara Jordan Publishing

7. Our Community / *Nuestra comunidad*

Name / Nombre

Activity 1 / *Actividad 1*

a. *Ordena las letras, para encontrar las cosas en inglés que algunas personas utilizan todos los días en sus trabajos. Intenta identificar cuales son sus ocupaciones.*

1. sokob   _____

2. shfle   _____   _____

1. roufl   _____

2. ragsu   _____   _____

1. lfweors   _____

2. treaw   _____   _____

b. Unscramble the letters to find things in Spanish that different people use every day at work. Then, try to figure out the corresponding occupation.

1. *outa*   _____

2. *solgaian*   _____   _____

1. *rofcominó*   _____

2. *caistnoi*   _____   _____

1. *emdinaci*   _____

2. *llacima*   _____   _____

water	sugar	flowers	shelf	books	flour
auto	camilla	micrófono	gasolina	noticias	medicina

Name / Nombre

Activity 2 / *Actividad 2*

Hunt through the word search below. When you find these words circle them.

Busca en la sopa de letras. Cuando encuentres las palabras al final de la página enciérralas.

C	O	N	D	U	C	T	O	R	D	S	M	N	N	G
O	B	U	T	D	O	C	E	P	O	L	I	C	I	A
M	P	I	C	O	V	X	B	A	C	Z	Q	R	W	R
P	O	L	I	C	E	M	A	N	R	O	T	C	O	D
N	L	M	B	T	J	P	K	Y	T	F	E	D	V	E
D	I	R	V	O	B	N	E	D	S	R	N	T	W	N
X	C	C	S	R	G	U	R	I	O	H	D	D	M	E
E	I	E	R	A	T	A	R	E	D	A	N	A	P	R
S	L	I	B	R	A	R	I	A	N	X	A	C	V	O
E	G	M	S	A	S	H	O	P	K	E	E	P	E	R
D	R	V	E	R	A	R	E	D	N	E	T	F	G	E
W	S	D	B	N	M	K	L	L	O	P	R	O	F	V
S	J	A	R	D	I	N	E	R	O	D	A	Q	E	I
S	C	T	R	T	S	I	L	A	N	R	U	O	J	R
P	E	R	I	O	D	I	S	T	A	F	G	V	R	D

driver	doctor	*periodista*
gardener	librarian	*tendera*
policeman	shopkeeper	*conductor*
baker	*panadera*	*policía*
journalist	*jardinero*	*doctora*

Bilingual Kids: English-Spanish, Vol. 2   © 2005 Sara Jordan Publishing

8. Opposites / *Los opuestos*

Activity 1 / *Actividad 1*

Color the picture and write down the opposites you see.

Colorea la imagen y escribe los opuestos que ves.

short / *bajo*   tall / *alto*

far / *lejos*

new / *nuevo*

old / *viejo*

close / *cerca*

small / *pequeño*   big / *grande*

1. _____   _____

2. _____   _____

3. _____   _____

4. _____   _____

Name / Nombre

Activity 1 / *Actividad 1*

How many opposites can you find? Try to find as many opposites as you can in Spanish with the letters in the fish tank. Write them down.

Trata de formar palabras opuestas en inglés con las letras que hay en el acuario. Escríbelas.

1. _____ / _____   6. _____ / _____

2. _____ / _____   7. _____ / _____

3. _____ / _____   8. _____ / _____

4. _____ / _____   9. _____ / _____

5. _____ / _____   10. _____ / _____

Activity 2 / *Actividad 2*

Look at the pictures and circle the "opposite" words on the right.

Observa las imágenes y encierra los opuestos a su derecha.

	thick	far	big
	grueso	lejos	grande

	night	day	old
	noche	*día*	*viejo*

	go	under	small
	siga	*debajo*	*pequeño*

	close	young	short
	cerca	*joven*	*bajo*

	empty	backward	heavy
	vacío	*atrás*	*pesado*

We measure things in many different ways.
Podemos medir las cosas en diferentes formas.

To measure time we use **a clock**.
*Para medir el tiempo usamos **el reloj**.*

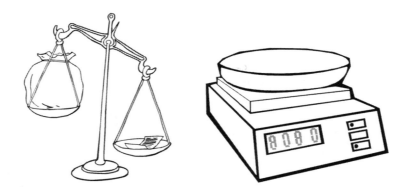

To measure weight we use **a scale**.
*Para medir el peso usamos **la balanza**.*

Bilingual Kids: English-Spanish, Vol. 2   © 2005 Sara Jordan Publishing

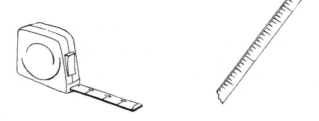

To measure length we use **a tape measure** or **a ruler.**
*Para medir la longitud usamos **el metro** o **la regla.***

To measure temperature we use **a thermometer.**
*Para medir la temperatura usamos **el termómetro.***

When we cook we can use **a spoon** or **a cup.**
*Cuando cocinamos podemos utilizar **la cuchara** o **la taza.***

Name / Nombre

Activity 1 / *Actividad 1*

Help Juan to complete the sentences in English and Spanish by choosing the correct measuring device. Write the name of each device on the lines below.

Ayúdale a Juan a completar las oraciones en inglés y en español, escogiendo el instrumento preciso. Escribe el nombre de cada instrumento.

1. Aunt Betty needs a _____ to measure the flour for her cake.

   La tía Betty necesita una _____ para medir la harina de su pastel.

2. I have to set the alarm on my _____ to wake up on time.

   Tengo que poner la alarma en mi _____ para levantarme a tiempo.

3. I weigh my turkey in kilograms or pounds with a _____.

   Yo peso mi pavo en kilogramos o en libras con una _____.

9. Measurement / *La medida*

Activity 2 / *Actividad 2*

Write the name of the measuring devices in English and Spanish.
Match them with the images on the table.

Escribe el nombre de los instrumentos en inglés y en español.
Relacionalos con las imágenes en la mesa.

1. _____/_____   4. _____/_____

2. _____/_____   5. _____/_____

3. _____/_____   6. _____/_____

The Sounds of *r* in Spanish / *Los sonidos de la r en español*

1. The soft sound of *r* is used whenever the single *r* (*ere*) appears in a word. (See exception on page 43.)

   *El sonido suave de la **r** se usa cada vez que aparece la **r** (ere) en una palabra. (Ver excepción en la página 43.)*

círculo

suéter

corazón

tren

mariposa

árbol

The soft sound of *r* is pronounced with a single flap of the tongue against the roof of the mouth.

*El sonido suave de la **r** se pronuncia con un solo golpe de la lengua contra el paladar.*

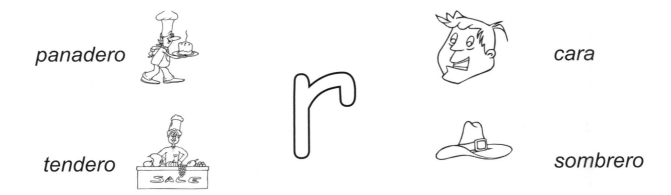

panadero

tendero

cara

sombrero

Bilingual Kids: English-Spanish, Vol. 2 © 2005 Sara Jordan Publishing

2. The strong sound of *r* is used when:
   *El sonido fuerte de la **r** se usa cuando:*

   a. the *rr* (*doble erre*) appears in a word.
      *la **rr** (doble erre) aparece en una palabra.*

guitarra

gorra

carreta

perro

   b. the single *r* appears at the beginning of a word or after an *l*, *m*, *n* or *s*.
      *la **r** aparece al principio de una palabra o después de **l**, **m**, **n** o **s**.*

Enrique

rosa

reloj

rata

The strong sound of *r* is pronounced with double flap of the tongue against the roof of the mouth. Roll up your tongue and make it flap rapidly.

*El sonido fuerte de la **r** se pronuncia con doble golpe de la lengua contra el paladar. Enrolla tu lengua y golpea el paladar rápidamente.*

Name / Nombre

Activity 1 / *Actividad 1*

Draw a line to match each picture to the correct sound.

Traza una línea para unir cada imagen con el sonido correspondiente.

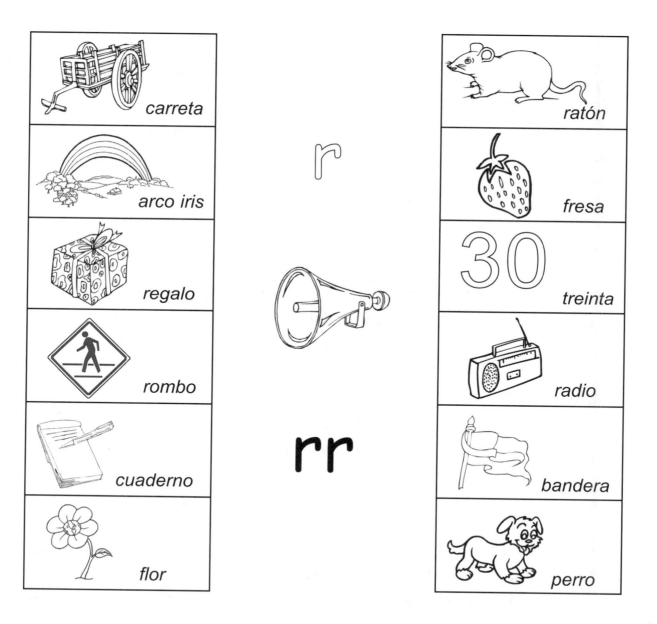

carreta

arco iris

regalo

rombo

cuaderno

flor

r

rr

ratón

fresa

treinta

radio

bandera

perro

Bilingual Kids: English-Spanish, Vol. 2   © 2005 Sara Jordan Publishing

10. The *r* and *rr* / *La r y la rr*

Activity 2 / *Actividad 2*

a. Circle, with yellow, the soft sound of *r*.
   Circle, with blue, the strong sound of *r*.

   *Encierra, con color amarillo, el sonido suave de la **r**.*
   *Encierra, con color azul, el sonido fuerte de la **r**.*

ropa	Enrique	araña
aro	reloj	refresco
amor	bombero	rana
río	nariz	garaje

b. Let's practice the pronunciation with this famous Spanish saying!

   ¡Practiquemos la pronunciación con este conocido refrán en español!

> **rr** con **rr** ciga**rr**o
> **rr** con **rr** ba**rr**il
> **r**ápido **r**uedan los ca**rr**os
> cargados de azúcar al fe**rr**oca**rr**il.

The English verb *to be* has two Spanish equivalents: *ser* and *estar*. They have distinct uses and are not interchangeable.

In Spanish, the verb *to be* is not used to express age. To express age one uses the verb *to have* (*tener*).

How old are you?   ¿Cuántos años tienes?

Let's conjugate the verb **ser**.

I am	yo soy
you are	tú eres / usted es
he is	él es
she is	ella es
we are	nosotros somos
you are	ustedes son / vosotros sois
they are	ellos son

He is tall.
Él es alto.

Los verbos **ser** *y* **estar** *son equivalentes a un mismo verbo en inglés:* **to be**. *Este es un verbo irregular y su significado se identifica según su contexto y estructura gramatical.*

El verbo **to be** *es usado en inglés para expresar la edad.*

How old are you?   ¿Cuántos años tienes?

Conjuguemos el verbo **estar**.

I am	yo estoy
you are	tú estás / usted está
he is	él está
she is	ella está
we are	nosotros estamos
you are	ustedes están / vosotros estáis
they are	ellos están

He is sad.
Él está triste.

11. *ser* and / *y estar*

Some ways we use *ser* / *Algunas formas de usar el verbo ser*

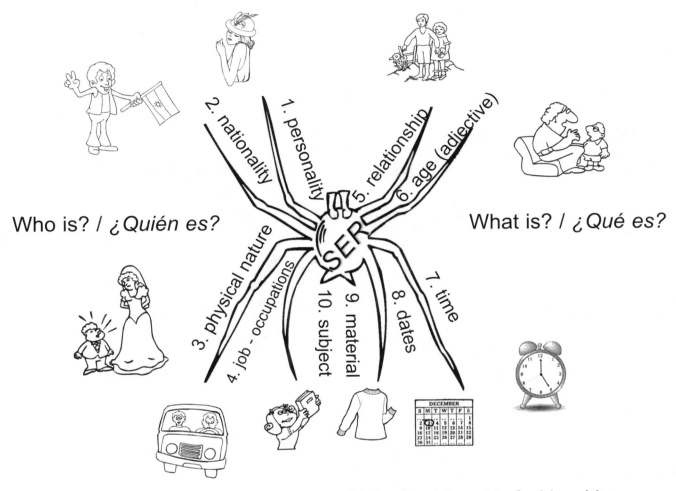

1. personality
2. nationality
3. physical nature
4. job - occupations
5. relationship
6. age (adjective)
7. time
8. dates
9. material
10. subject

Who is? / ¿Quién es?

What is? / ¿Qué es?

SER

1. *La señorita Rodríguez es elegante.* / Miss Rodríguez is fashionable.

2. *El señor Pérez es de Argentina.* / Mr. Pérez is from Argentina.

3. *Ana es alta y Pedro es bajo.* / Ana is tall and Pedro is short.

4. *Felipe es conductor.* / Felipe is a driver.

5. *Juan y Daniela son hermanos.* / Juan and Daniela are brother and sister.

6. *Ella es anciana y él es joven.* / She is old and he is young.

7. *Son las 5:00 de la tarde.* / It is 5:00 pm.

8. *Hoy es el 3 de diciembre.* / Today is December 3rd.

9. *El suéter es de lana.* / The sweater is made of wool.

10. *El libro es de Juliana.* / It is Juliana's book.

Bilingual Kids: English-Spanish, Vol. 2   © 2005 Sara Jordan Publishing

47

Estar expresses transitory qualities. / *Estar* expresa cualidades transitorias.

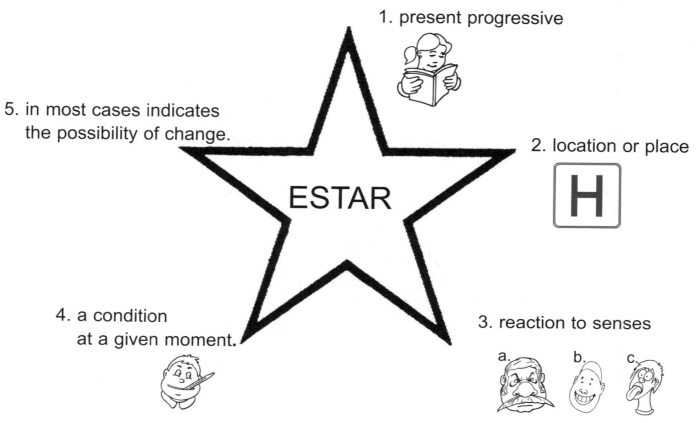

1. present progressive

5. in most cases indicates the possibility of change.

ESTAR

2. location or place

H

4. a condition at a given moment.

3. reaction to senses

a. b. c.

1. *Lucía está leyendo.* / Lucía is reading.

2. *El Dr. Flórez está en el hospital.* / Dr. Flórez is at the hospital.

3. a. *El abuelo está enojado.* / Grandpa is upset.

   b. *David está feliz.* / David is happy now.

   d. *La carne está salada.* / The meat is salty.

4. *Pedro está enfermo.* / Pedro is sick.

5. *Gloria está cansada.* / Gloria is tired.

Bilingual Kids: English-Spanish, Vol. 2   © 2005 Sara Jordan Publishing

11. *ser* and / y *estar*

Name / Nombre

Activity 1 / *Actividad 1*

Fill in the blanks with the correct form of the verbs *ser* and *estar*.

Llena los espacios con la forma correcta de los verbos **ser** *y* **estar**.

1) a. Juan _es_ mexicano.

   b. Joe _____ ____ Canadá.

   c. Ellos _____ amigos.

2) a. Pedro _____ bajo.

   b. Ana _____ alta.

   c. Ellos _____ enamorados.

3) a. El Dr. Flórez _____ en el hospital.

   b. Andrea _____ enferma.

4) a. Hoy _____ el 3 de diciembre.

   b. _____ las ocho de la mañana.

Name / Nombre

Actividad 2 / *Activity 2*

Read the descriptions below and label the pictures by letter. ie. a, b, c.
Lee las descripciones y escribe en cada imagen la letra correspondiente.

a. *Ellos son reyes. Ellos son ancianos.*
   They are King and Queen. They are elderly.

b. *Él es de Brasil. Él es futbolista. Él está pateando el balón.*
   He is from Brazil. He is a football player. He is kicking the ball.

c. *Él es un personaje de caricaturas. Él es muy travieso. Él está sonriendo.*
   He is a cartoon character. He is very naughty. He is smiling.

d. *Ella es cantante. Ella es colombiana. Ella es rubia.*
   She is a singer. She is Colombian. She is blond.

e. *Él es un personaje de las tiras cómicas. Él es poderoso.*
   He is a character in the comics. He is powerful.

f. *Ella es una niña. Ella es joven. Ella está caminando.*
   She is a little girl. She is young. She is walking.

Bilingual Kids: English-Spanish, Vol. 2   © 2005 Sara Jordan Publishing

12. *conocer* and / y *saber*

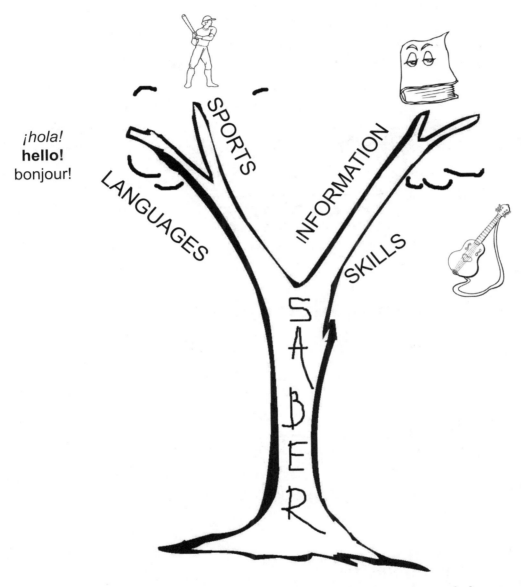

¡hola!
hello!
bonjour!

Let's Conjugate It! / ¡Conjuguémoslo!

I know	*yo sé*
you know	*tú sabes / usted sabe*
he knows	*él sabe*
she knows	*ella sabe*
we know	*nosotros sabemos*
you know	*ustedes saben / vosotros sabéis*
they know	*ellos saben*

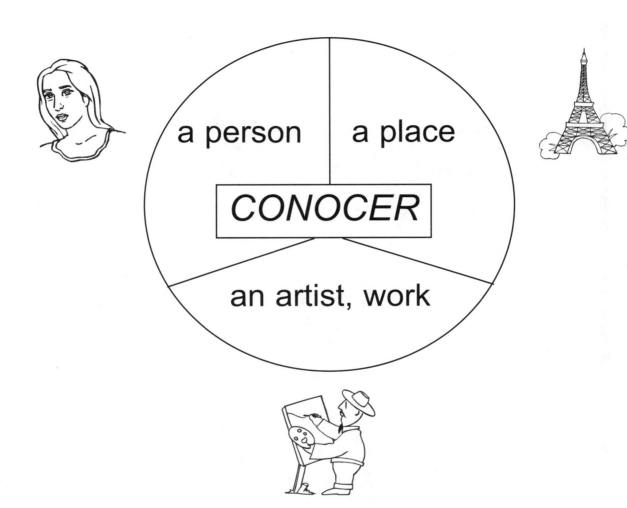

Let's Conjugate It! / *¡Conjuguémoslo!*

I know	*yo conozco*
you know	*tú conoces / usted conoce*
he knows	*él conoce*
she knows	*ella conoce*
we know	*nosotros conocemos*
you know	*ustedes conocen / vosotros conocéis*
they know	*ellos conocen*

12. *conocer* and / y *saber*

Activity 1 / *Activity 1*

a. Find and circle the words that <u>are</u> <u>not</u> a form of *saber* or *conocer*.

*Encierra las palabras que <u>no</u> <u>son</u> una forma de los verbos **saber** o **conocer**.*

sabes	conozco	sabe	suben
comeréis	subo	conoce	sabemos

b. Use the verbs below (*yo sé* and *yo conozco*) and write the number of the images in the correct column.

*Utiliza los verbos siguientes (**yo sé** y **yo conozco**) y escribe el número de las imágenes en la columna correcta.*

1. tocar guitarra	Yo sé...	Yo conozco...	4. los poemas de Neruda
2. las pinturas de Picasso			5. jugar al fútbol
3. a Camilo			6. Italia

Name / Nombre

Activity 2 / *Actividad 2*

You are in Peru and want to send a postcard to your family. Complete the sentences with the correct form of the verbs: *ser*, *estar*, *saber* and *conocer*. Use the word box.

*Tú estás en Perú y quieres enviar una postal a tu familia. Completa las frases con la forma correcta de los verbos: **ser**, **estar**, **saber** y **conocer** Usa las palabras al final de la página.*

Querida Familia:

Yo_____ feliz aquí en América del Sur.

Ya _____ el Perú, Bolivia y Ecuador.

Estos países _____ muy bonitos. La gente

_____ muy amable. Mis nuevos amigos

Rubén y Claudia _____ hablar español.

Ellos _____ hoy en la playa porque el

día _____ soleado.

Yo ya _____ cocinar el cebiche peruano.

¡Delicioso!

_____
(escribe tu nombre aquí)

Perú, América del Sur.

es	*sé*	*son*
está	*estoy*	*conozco*
están	*saben*	

Bilingual Kids: English-Spanish, Vol. 2   © 2005 Sara Jordan Publishing

Review / *Repaso*

Name / Nombre

Review / *Repaso*

1. Complete the word with the appropiate vowel or article.

la arañ__   el zapat__   __ __ abeja   el och__

__ __ mesa   __ __ niña   __ __ auto   __ __ lunes

2. Write the corresponding numbers in English and Spanish.

10 _____ / _____   20 _____ / _____

30 _____ / _____   60 _____ / _____

3. Fill in the blanks by translating the English words into Spanish.

circle _____   square _____

rhombus _____   rectangle _____

4. Fill in the blanks using the correct form of **saber** or **conocer**.

a. Yo _____ España.

b. Mi profesora _____ hablar inglés.

c. Mis abuelos _____ tocar piano.

d. Mis amigos _____ las playas de Cuba.

e. Yo _____ hablar español.

Bilingual Kids: English-Spanish, Vol. 2   © 2005 Sara Jordan Publishing

55

Page 12 / Activity 1

la eme   *el* ocho   *el* rojo
                         el amarillo
                         el verde

la mujer   *el* sombrero   *el* cero

la luna   *la* eñe   *el* lunes

Page 13 / Activity 2

a) *(el)*   *(la)*
   1. *tío*   1. *mujer*
   2. *trece*   2. red
   3. *él*   3. *oreja*
   4. *eco*   4. *osa*
   5. *lunes*   5. *abeja*
   6. *sol*   6. *eme*

b)   *la araña*   *el zapato*
      la mesa   *el auto*

Page 16 / Activity 1

a.   two
      four
      twenty-one
      thirty

b.   *siete*
      veintinueve
      quince
      treinta

Page 17 / Activity 2

tres / three + *nueve* / nine
= *doce* / twelve

trece / thirteen + *siete* / seven
= *veinte* / twenty

cinco / five + *ocho* / eight
= *trece* / thirteen

Page 20 / Activity 1

T	E	N	S	E	T	E	N	T	A	X	O	O
T	R	E	I	N	T	A	Z	N	E	I	C	N
S	E	V	E	N	T	Y	B	W	C	F	H	E
C	I	N	C	U	E	N	T	A	A	T	E	H
Q	G	D	Y	V	T	H	I	R	T	Y	N	U
M	H	K	L	N	W	R	L	P	N	N	T	N
S	T	N	I	N	E	T	Y	B	E	O	A	D
X	Y	H	R	F	N	G	Q	P	R	V	Y	R
S	E	S	E	N	T	A	S	D	A	E	T	E
Z	F	O	R	T	Y	X	W	R	U	N	F	D
S	E	T	N	I	E	V	I	F	C	T	I	W
D	I	E	Z	S	Y	T	X	I	S	A	F	G

Bilingual Kids: English-Spanish, Vol. 2   © 2005 Sara Jordan Publishing

Page 21 / Activity 2

twenty / *veinte*

thirty / *treinta*

sixty / *sesenta*

one hundred / *cien*

Page 24 / Activity 1

a.

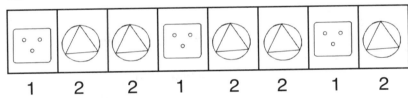

1   2   2   1   2   2   1   2

b.   square   *cuadrado*
       triangle   *triángulo*
       circle   *círculo*

Page 25 / Activity 2

```
        C                 A        C
 L      I      G       A N C H O   O
 A      R      R          G        R
 R E C T A N G U L O      O        T
 G      U      A          S        O
 O      L      N          T
        O      D       R O M B O
               E
```

Page 27 / Activity 1

We are bored.
Nosotros estamos aburridos.

They are surprised.
Ellos están sorprendidos.

You are happy.
Tú estás feliz.

He is angry.
Él está enojado.

Page 30 / Activity 1

1. *los cerdos*	2. *los caballos*	3. *las mariposas*
4. *los soles*	5. *las vacas*	6. *los árboles*
7. *las flores*	8. *las gallinas*	9. *los patos*

Page 31 / Activity 2

a. cow / *la vaca*

b. hen / *la gallina*

c. goat / *la cabra*

Page 33 / Activity 1

a)
1. books
2. shelf   librarian

1. flour
2. sugar   baker

1. flowers
2. water   gardener

b)
1. *auto*
2. *gasolina*   *conductor(a)*

1. *micrófono*
2. *noticias*   *periodista*

1. *medicina*
2. *camilla*   *doctor(a)*

Page 34 / Activity 2

Page 34 / Activity 2

1. small / big
   pequeño / grande

2. short / tall
   bajo / alto

3. far / close
   lejos / cerca

4. new / old
   nuevo / viejo

Bilingual Kids: English-Spanish, Vol. 2 © 2005 Sara Jordan Publishing

Answer Keys / *Respuestas*

Page 36 / Activity 1

1. far / close
2. small / big
3. old / new
4. wide / narrow
5. black white

1. *lejos /cerca*
2. *pequeño / grande*
3. *viejo / nuevo*
4. *ancho / angosto*
5. *blanco / negro*

Page 37 / Activity 1

1. thick / *grueso*

2. day / *día*

3. go / *siga*

4. young / *joven*

5. empty / *vacío*

Page 40 / Activity 1

1. c) cup
       taza

2. a) clock
       reloj

3. d) scale
       balanza

Page 41 / Activity 2

1. clock / *reloj*

2. scale / *balanza*

3. cup / *taza*

4. tape measure / *metro*

5. spoon / *cuchara*

6. thermometer / *termómetro*

Page 44 / Activity 1

r sound (ere)
arco iris
cuaderno
flor
bandera
treinta
fresa

rr sound (erre)
carreta
regalo
rombo
ratón
radio
perro

Page 45 / Activity 5

Yellow:

aro	*amor*	*bombero*
nariz	*araña*	*garaje*
refresco		

Blue:

ropa	*río*	*Enrique*
reloj	*refresco*	*rana*

Page 49 / Activity 1

a) *Juan es mexicano*
b) *es de*
c) *son*

a) *es*
b) *es*
c) *están*

a) *está*
b) *está*

a) *es*
b) *Son*

Page 50 / Activity 2

Answer Keys / *Respuestas*

Page 53 / Activity 1

a) *suben / comeréis / subo*

b)   *Yo sé*
       1 / 5

       Yo conozco
       2 / 3 / 4 / 6

Page 54 / Activity 2

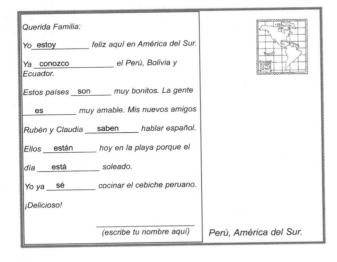

Page 55 / Activity 2

1. *la araña   el zapato   la abeja   el ocho*

   la mesa   la niña   el auto   el lunes

2. 10 ten / diez   20 twenty / veinte

   30 thirty / treinta   60 sixty / sesenta

3. circle círculo   square cuadrado

   rhombus rombo   rectangle rectángulo

4. a. *conozco*
   b. *sabe*
   c. *saben*
   d. *conocen*
   e. *sé*

About Sara Jordan Publishing

Sara Jordan Publishing, a recognized leader in the development of high quality educational materials, has been producing audio/book kits designed to improve literacy, numeracy, language skills (English, French and Spanish), self-esteem and interest in the world's diverse cultures, since 1990. These award-winning programs are recommended by teachers and parents and enjoyed worldwide.

Bilingual Songs: English-Spanish, vol. 1 Exciting songs in both English and Spanish teach the alphabet, counting to 10, days of the week, months of the year, weather, seasons, colors, food, animals at the zoo, parts of the body, clothing and family members. Music accompaniment tracks make class performances a snap! Includes lyrics/activity book. Our new companion resource book, ***Bilingual Kids: English-Spanish, vol. 1***, comes complete with reproducible lessons and activities based on the songs.

Bilingual Songs: English-Spanish, vol. 2 Hip songs in English and Spanish teach counting to 30, counting by tens, shapes and sizes, emotions, places in the community, opposites, measuring devices, pronunciation of R and RR, conocer and saber, ser and estar. Music accompaniment tracks make class performances a snap! Includes lyrics/activity book. Our new companion resource book, ***Bilingual Kids: English-Spanish, vol. 2***, comes complete with reproducible lessons and activities based on the songs.

Bilingual Songs: English-Spanish, vol. 3 These 12 upbeat bilingual songs teach: greetings, gender, articles, plural forms of nouns, numbers, capitalization, adjectives, common phrases and much more! Sung in both Spanish and English by native speakers. Music accompaniment tracks make class performances a snap! Includes lyrics/activity book. Our new companion resource book, ***Bilingual Kids: English-Spanish, vol. 3***, comes complete with reproducible lessons and activities based on the songs.

Bilingual Songs: English-Spanish, vol. 4 Spanish is a snap with these 12 catchy tunes teaching: pronouns, gender exceptions, the verb 'estar', adverbs of frequency, question words, comparative and superlative adjectives, and much more! Music accompaniment tracks make class performances a snap! Includes lyrics/activity book. Our new companion resource book, ***Bilingual Kids: English-Spanish, vol. 4***, comes complete with reproducible lessons and activities based on the songs.

Español para principiantes Great for beginners! Teaches the alphabet, farm animals, counting, family members, parts of the body, days of the week, colors, fruit, opposites and shapes in Spanish. The accompanying lyrics/activity book has fun assignments and crossword puzzles! Music accompaniment tracks make class performances a snap! Our new companion resource book, **Spanish for Kids: Beginning Lessons**, comes complete with reproducible lessons and activities based on the songs.

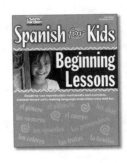

Canciones temáticas para aprender idiomas Fun songs and activities for beginners of Spanish. Themes include: salutations, rooms in the house, pets, meals, food, transportation, communication, parts of the body, clothing and the weather. The lyrics book includes exercises which may be reproduced by the classroom teacher. Our new companion resource book, **Spanish for Kids: Thematic Lessons**, comes complete with reproducible lessons and activities based on the songs.

Fonética funky... y algo más Students love to learn Spanish with Rap! They'll learn the alphabet, vowels, consonants, telling time, days of the week, months of the year, seasons, about the environment and more! Includes reproducible lyrics book.

Gramática rítmica Ten upbeat Spanish grammar songs that teach basic grammar rules: nous, pronouns, adjectives, and the conjugation of verbs in present and past tenses. Exciting exercises and crossword puzzles are included in the lyrics book. A complement of 10 "music-only" accompaniment tracks allows students to perform karaoke style.

Conjugación en canción Entertaining songs in Spanish teach conjugations of high frequency verbs in the present, preterit and future tenses, including irregular verbs. The accompanying lyrics/activity book includes exciting exercises.

Bilingual Songs: English-French, vol. 1 Learn in both English and French, the alphabet, counting to 10, days of the week, months of the year, weather, seasons, colors, food, animals at the zoo, parts of the body, clothing and family members. A bonus of music accompaniment tracks make class performances a snap! Lyrics/activity book included. Our new companion resource book, **Bilingual Kids: English-French, vol. 1**, comes complete with reproducible lessons and activities based on the songs.

Bilingual Songs: English-French, vol. 2 Hip songs in English and French that teach counting to 30, counting by tens, shapes, sizes, emotions, places in the community, opposites and measuring devices. Includes music accompaniment tracks for class performances. The accompanying lyrics book includes activities which may be photocopied by the classroom teacher. Our new companion resource book, **Bilingual Kids: English-French, vol. 2**, comes complete with reproducible lessons and activities based on the songs.

Bilingual Songs: English-French, vol. 3 Twelve upbeat, bilingual songs teach: greetings, gender, articles, plural forms of nouns, cardinal and ordinal numbers, descriptive adjectives, punctuation, common phrases and much more! Music accompaniment tracks make class performances a snap! Lyrics/activity book included. Our new companion resource book, **Bilingual Kids: English-French, vol. 3**, comes complete with reproducible lessons and activities based on the songs.

Bilingual Songs: English-French, vol. 4 Snappy songs teach: pronouns, gender exceptions, the verb 'être', adverbs, adjectives, punctuation, question words and much more! Sung in both French and English by native speakers. A complement of music accompaniment tracks can be used for class performances. The lyrics book may be photocopied by the teacher. Our new companion resource book, **Bilingual Kids: English-French, vol. 4**, comes complete with reproducible lessons and activities based on the songs.

Join our community...

We would like to invite you to join the online community of teachers, parents, friends and associates who receive our electronic newsletter. Every two weeks we faithfully write up teaching ideas, related links and lesson plans based on one, two and sometimes even three of our songs. These are all sent, free of charge, along with the free song downloads to recipients of our newsletter. We feel that parents and teachers find them very valuable.

To subscribe to our free newsletter in English or Spanish please visit www.SongsThatTeach.com or www.Aprendecantando.com. To receive a free copy of our catalog please call 1-800-567-7733.